I0447208

SSI ERAP Monograph

REBUILDING ARMED FORCES:
LEARNING FROM IRAQ AND LEBANON

Florence Gaub

May 2011

*****

Comments pertaining to this report are invited and should be forwarded to: Director, Strategic Studies Institute, U.S. Army War College, 632 Wright Ave, Carlisle, PA 17013-5046.

*****

This manuscript was funded by the U.S. Army War College External Research Associates Program. Information on this program is available on our website, *www.StrategicStudiesInstitute. army.mil*, at the Publishing button.

*****

All Strategic Studies Institute (SSI) publications may be downloaded free of charge from the SSI website. Hard copies of this report may also be obtained free of charge while supplies last by placing an order on the SSI website. The SSI website address is: *www.StrategicStudiesInstitute.army.mil*.

*****

The Strategic Studies Institute publishes a monthly e-mail newsletter to update the national security community on the research of our analysts, recent and forthcoming publications, and upcoming conferences sponsored by the Institute. Each newsletter also provides a strategic commentary by one of our research analysts. If you are interested in receiving this newsletter, please subscribe on the SSI website at *www.StrategicStudiesInstitute. army.mil/newsletter/*.

FOREWORD

Since U.S. operations began in Iraq in 2003, the Iraqi armed forces have embarked on a huge transformation. In this groundbreaking monograph, Dr. Florence Gaub focuses on the structural and sociological aspects of rebuilding the Iraqi armed forces, which she observes and comments on through the lens of lessons learned from Lebanon's experience of rebuilding its own armed forces in the late 20th century following civil war.

Given Iraq's geopolitical potential, this observation and commentary is especially important. Gaub's objectives in writing this monograph are to learn from past mistakes observed in both Iraq and Lebanon, highlighting possible ways to avoid making such mistakes in the future, and to offer recommendations for improving performance in future post-conflict situations.

Gaub focuses on the importance of fair and equal ethnic representation in the military and the presentation of a positive public image of the new military as a symbol of strength and justice within the nation. In addition, she notes the value that proper training of new recruits and integration of compromised elites and soldiers into the new armed forces have on strengthening bonds between soldiers and officers in a multiethnic, post-conflict army.

This monograph is an important contribution to the debate over how multiethnic armies in post-conflict situations should be rebuilt and to what degree societal unrest and public opinion influence the success of such undertakings.

DOUGLAS C. LOVELACE, JR.
Director
Strategic Studies Institute

ABOUT THE AUTHOR

FLORENCE GAUB is a Researcher and Lecturer in the North Atlantic Treaty Organization (NATO) Defence College's Middle East Faculty. Her areas of interest include the Arab world, military sociology, post-conflict reconstruction, and intercultural communication. Previously, she has served as a research fellow in the German Parliament, focusing on issues of defense, internal security and development. She has also held positions with the French Defence Ministry's Research Centre in the Social Sciences of Defence (*Centre d'études en sciences sociales de la defense*), the Centre for Security Studies in Sarajevo, the Centre for Applied Policy Research in Munich, as well as with the United Nations Institute for Training and Research in New York, where she coordinated courses for diplomats posted at the United Nations. She has conducted extensive field studies in Lebanon, Iraq, Nigeria, and Bosnia-Herzegovina. She has published several articles and two books on these topics, and has lectured widely with The NATO School, Oberammergau, Germany; Allied Joint Forces Command Naples; and several think tanks and universities in the Middle East, Europe, and the United States. Dr. Gaub graduated from Sorbonne University in Paris, France, and the Ludwig-Maximilians-University in Munich, Germany, and holds a Ph.D. from the Department of Political Science at Humboldt University of Berlin.

SUMMARY

Rebuilding a foreign security force after a conflict requires more than technical know-how: it requires cultural and historical knowledge; an understanding of the conflict; and, most importantly, awareness of the place of the new military in post-conflict society. We need not only establish guidelines for what we can do, but must also realize the limits to this endeavor.

The following analysis summarizes the experiences of two different states that had to rebuild their armed forces in the aftermath of a conflict: Iraq and Lebanon. Both cases are untapped sources of experiences and lessons that provide insight into the region's evolving military structure.

The monograph focuses more on structural and sociological aspects and less on technical ones. The main objectives are to outline the special situation of a military force in a post-conflict setting, to learn from two cases in order to avoid past mistakes, and to improve future performance in the rebuilding of foreign armed forces. The analysis follows five lines: the ethnic make-up of the armed forces, the recruitment process, the inclusion or exclusion of politically compromised personnel, the image of the military in society, and the professionalization of the new force. All five areas are especially delicate to handle in a volatile post-conflict environment.

Ethnic composition of the armed forces is always a challenge for multiethnic states and is especially difficult in a post-conflict situation. Where the composition of the military is based on access to wealth, position, and education, it might well become the symbol of a situation of discontent that is part of the conflict.

Reversing this order is thus crucial if future conflicts are to be avoided. There are two ways to influence the military's ethnic composition: as part of the recruitment process (which will be explained further in the monograph) and within the existing body. The latter is extremely difficult because it means interfering with an institution that resents political meddling and would entail either fast-tracking new personnel or dismissing others.

The challenge is less pronounced when it comes to entry into the armed forces. While applying a quota to the recruits might be undesirable, it is less so when combined with strong meritocratic principles. The remaining question then is the kind of quota — should it be ethnic, religious, or possibly regional? The former two bear the danger of institutionalizing religion or ethnicity within the military, yet by the same token, they ensure equal representation of all groups concerned. Rebalancing a military force according to ethnic affiliation might create intra-corps jealousy, distorted chains of commands following the ethnic rather than the official order, fragile cohesion, and possibly disobedience.

Both the Iraqi and the Lebanese cases highlight both the desire for ethnically-balanced armed forces in a post-conflict setting and the political attempts that frequently will forego moral concerns in order to achieve this goal. Thus, policymakers involved in rebuilding armed forces in a multiethnic setting should aim at a fair balance of all ethnic groups within the military and pay close attention to nondiscrimination for all groups.

Another delicate issue is the inclusion or exclusion of personnel who are deemed politically undesirable. This can include former regime members or militiamen. The problem here is that in the former case, elites usually carry the know-how, the intellectual capacity, and the institutional memory necessary to rebuild a state and its institutions. Excluding them from the rebuilding process can not only slow down the process, but also create a pool of frustrated personnel opposing the new state. The same is true for the disbandment of former militias. Rebuilding states thus have to choose between moral and practical considerations.

In addition to addressing the makeup of the new armed forces, it is also imperative to discuss the public image the new organization has or should have. Whether or not the armed forces will be able to serve society depends to a large extent on their relationship with it. An armed force despised and distrusted by the society it belongs to may have difficulties establishing cohesion and legitimacy; the Lebanese case supports that contention, whereas the Iraqi case provides contrary evidence.

This is related, though not exclusively, to the military's professionalism, which determines the commitment, skill, and discipline of military personnel and is also considered an antidote to many problems that plague post-conflict countries, such as preventing the military's intervention into politics, mutiny, and disintegration. In a post-conflict situation, military professionalism is thus not only desperately needed, but has usually been adversely affected by the conflict years, especially when sectarianism tested loyalties and cohesion.

This is true both for Iraq and Lebanon, but the two countries differ greatly when it comes to the reestablishment of professionalism. While the Lebanese armed forces had, and have, an ideology that inspires military professionalism called *Shehabism* (after its first Commander-in-Chief, Fuad Shehab), the Iraqi army not only emerged much more affected from decades of dictatorship, but also currently lacks such a glue to hold it all together; a national ideology and identity. Yet, an armed force that has no identity will have difficulty providing its men with a sense of duty to nation and country, creating cohesion and commitment. While skill and discipline might be trainable, the nontangible elements of military professionalism have to come from within the society and institution in order to be as powerful as needed.

Professionalization of a military force relies mostly on an inner logic that needs to be intrinsic; a sense of purpose, duty, and belonging to a nation that requires education, which must come from within. It is for this reason that the military is frequently associated with nationalism. An armed force that has no devotion, no sense of duty to its nation, will find it very difficult to stand together in times of war and conflict independently from the amount of training.

Rebuilding armed forces while ignoring these five dimensions means rebuilding it only partly; a military institution that represents only one part of society, that stands for sectarianism rather than unity, that lacks capacity and professionalism, and most importantly a vision of its mission, will never be able to truly fulfill its role.

REBUILDING ARMED FORCES: LEARNING FROM IRAQ AND LEBANON

Introduction.

Although the reconstruction of armed forces after a conflict is not novel— just think of the German Bundeswehr or Japanese military—the methods for doing so have increased in importance and visibility with the advent of state-building in general, and security sector reform in particular, after the end of the Cold War. While there is now widespread agreement that capable security forces are at the center of post-conflict reconstruction, very few lessons-learned analyses exist, and in consequence, our understanding of how armed forces are to be rebuilt is still imperfect. We need to establish not only guidelines for what we can do, but also realize the limits to this endeavor. Rebuilding a foreign security force after a conflict requires more than technical know-how: it requires cultural and historical knowledge, an understanding of the conflict and, most importantly, of the place of the new military in post-conflict society.

Both Iraq and Lebanon are two useful cases to learn from when it comes to the reconstruction of the armed forces in a post-conflict scenario, irrespective of their actual military performance on the battlefield. The following analyses summarize the experiences these two different states had in rebuilding their armed forces in the aftermath of a conflict. While Lebanon reformed and rebuilt its scattered and destroyed army largely without international assistance, Iraq had, and continues to have, support from organizations and countries as diverse as the North Atlantic Treaty Organization (NATO) and Iran. Both cases are untapped sources of experiences and lessons and provide insights into the region's evolving military structure.

The challenge of rebuilding armed forces in a post-conflict setting will be analyzed along several lines that not only allow comparison, but also deepen the understanding of the challenges that the national military institution faces after an internal conflict. These include representation of the different communities within the armed forces, and most notably the officer corps; the ways of recruitment into the new military; the inclusion or exclusion of former enemy combatants or personnel who are politically compromised; the public perception of the institution as such; and ways and means of professionalization.

The study focuses mostly on structural and sociological aspects and less on technical ones because it is in these areas that the knowledge is underdeveloped, whereas technical military cooperation has already been widely studied. The main objectives are to outline the special situation of a military force in a post-conflict setting, to learn from two cases so as to avoid past mistakes, and to improve future performance in the rebuilding of foreign armed forces.

A Plural Armed Force? Ethnic Representation in the Military.

Armed forces in plural societies face a particular challenge: while most state institutions, especially those in the security sector, usually prefer to recruit proportionally more soldiers from groups deemed loyal to the state and regime, an exaggerated unbalance can create political unrest or even lead to the break-up of the very country. Such cases as Pakistan, where the underrepresentation of Bengalis in the armed forces ultimately led to the secession of Bangladesh, or Nigeria, where the over-representation of Ibos in the officer corps contributed to the Biafra-War, show clearly the symbolic value that many groups attach to the military, and more importantly, the officer corps.

Yet states need security and loyalty in the military sector more than they need social peace, so it seems quite logical that they prefer to recruit from groups known to be trustworthy. Unbalanced officer corps in ethnic or religious terms are thus rather frequent in multiethnic states and sometimes mirror social stratification in terms of access to education, wealth, and support for the state as such.

In the same vein, the pre-2003 Iraqi officer corps was 80 percent Arab Sunni Muslim (as was Saddam Hussein), mostly from tribes loyal to him such as the al-Ubaydi, Dulaim, and Jabour (of which, the latter two included Shi'a as well as Sunni). The remaining 20 percent were, after a large-scale purge of Kurdish officers, mostly Arab Shi'a.[1] Yet, this number stood in stark contrast to the composition of Iraq's society, which contains about 15-20 percent Sunni Arabs, 60 percent Shi'a Arabs, and 18 percent Kurds. Sunni Arabs were thus overly present in the officer corps, while the rank and file consisted of 80 percent Shi'a Arabs. It is important to note, however, that Shi'a Arab discrimination in the officer corps did not start with the regime of Saddam Hussein; rather, Shi'a were underrepresented traditionally in the Ottoman Army officer corps and in the early Iraqi armed forces as well. Limited access to the military academy, appointment to unattractive branches, posts in the Kurdish North, and mistreatment by Sunni officers were symptoms of the officer corps' disregard for the large numbers of Shi'a soldiers amidst their ranks.[2] Suspected by Sunni

Arabs to constitute a fifth column because of their different sect, (suspicions that were never confirmed, not even during the war against Iran), the Shi'a struggled to portray themselves as Iraqi nationalists. Shi'a troops were, however, present in in the rank and file.

Similar traits can be found in Lebanon, where the 1975 pre-civil war officer corps contained 58 percent Christian Maronites—a mild improvement from the 64 percent a decade earlier.[3] The Maronites, a small Catholic sect mostly residing in Lebanon, were at the forefront of Lebanese independence from Syria in 1943 and constituted the young state's prime supporters, as opposed to the Sunni, who favored a pan-Arab construct. Due to their strong investment in the state, their wealth, and their literacy, they dominated all state institutions and were overrepresented in the officer corps, even in the predecessor of the Lebanese Army, the French *Troupes Spéciales du Levant* (Special Troups of the Levant). By contrast, approximately 60 percent of the rank and file were traditionally Shi'a.

It is important to understand that under-representation in the armed forces can express several aspects of the relationship between society and the state: while some groups are traditionally more focused on other, better-paid professions, others shun the military because they do not identify with the state. By the same token, the state itself might discriminate against some groups suspected of fragile loyalty.

On the other hand, over-representation in the armed forces can be the expression of a particularly dire economic situation that pushed young men into governmental rather than business positions. Where the educational requirements for the officer corps are not met, however, the absence of a certain group in the officer corps will express first and foremost social stratification. Absence of Shi'a in the Lebanese officer corps, for instance, was mostly due to their difficulty in passing the tests (hence was an expression of social stratification), while absence of Iraqi Shi'a was an expression of the state's suspicion of their loyalty.

Social conflict, however, is in one way or another a symptom of discontent over the distribution of wealth, education, and position within a particular society, which is why one of its expressions is frequently a dispute over the composition of the armed forces. It is for this reason that both Iraq and Lebanon attempted to depart from this distortion by introducing post-conflict measures to balance the military. The end of the conflict thus equates with the end of ethnic and religious unbalance of the armed forces, and especially within the officer corps, because social peace suddenly equates with state security – the civil war in Lebanon, as the insurgency in Iraq questioned the state to the extent that it threatened its very existence. Finding a balance among all parties concerned suddenly ranks high on the state's agenda, and so does ethnic balancing in the armed forces.

There are two levels on which ethnic balancing takes place: upon recruitment (which will be treated further below) and within the existing body of the armed forces. Evidently, it is easier to balance an armed force built from scratch, but neither the Iraqi nor the Lebanese military were raised from zero. Rather, both forces effectively relied on the pre-war armed forces and thus inherited in part the ethnic and religious composition of the pre-war military. The problem with this kind of balancing is that it means interference with an existing body of troops who, in professional terms, usually resent political interference and to some extent value meritocratic principles (although the latter is not always the case in our two examples). Both Iraq and Lebanon reacted to the need to balance the armed forces, but in different ways.

The Lebanese Army, for instance, decided to reintegrate about 3,000 Christians who had fought with a renegade wing of the army under General Michel Awn because it could not afford to lose such a high number of well-trained units, but more importantly because it would have affected its religious balance.[4] In order to publicly assure religious equilibrium in the armed forces, it also institutionalized a Military Council staffed with six representatives of Lebanon's main religious groups as the army command, which soon earned the nickname *Conseil Confessionnel* (Confessional Council). Furthermore, the military created a complicated system which ensures equal distribution of command posts that, like a Rubik's cube, creates a horizontal and vertical balance of religious groups. If the commander of one company is Sunni, his assistant has to be a Christian, say a Greek Orthodox. In this case, the commander of the brigade should be a Christian, but not a Greek Orthodox, e.g., a Maronite.

The Iraqi military, in turn, has reemerged as an armed force largely resembling the old Iraqi armed forces (aside the junior officer ranks), containing a rather large share of Sunni Arabs in its officer corps[5] and Shi'a Arabs in the rank and file. The reason for this is simple: 70 percent of the officers are drawn from the largely Sunni Arab pre-war officer corps,[6] in spite of debaathification programs originally designed to dismiss any officer above the rank of colonel, and an unknown number of enlisted troops have likewise served in the old Iraqi military.[7] The need for experienced personnel, as well as the need for Sunni Arabs, finally overtook ethnic, moral, and religious concerns, so the new Iraqi armed forces contain a larger share of Sunni Arabs in their senior officer ranks, while the junior ranks correspond approximately to the believed share of each group in the population: 60 percent Shi'a Arab, 30 percent Sunni Arab, and 18 percent Kurds.[8]

Despite this top-heavy Sunni Arab share of officer positions, political attempts were made to balance senior ranks vertically as well as horizontally. Thus, the second post-2003 Minister of Defense, Abdul Qadr, was a Sunni Arab; Iraqi Armed Forces Chief of Staff Babakir Zebari, a Kurd; and his deputy, Nasier Abadi, a Shi'a Arab. Previously, a similar balance had existed, with the chief of staff being a Sunni Arab and his deputy being a Shi'a. All of these had served in the pre-2003 military. Similar balances exist for the divisional commanders, while the Iraqi Navy is under the command of a Shi'a, and the air force is under the command of a Kurd.[9] Overall, the distribution of the highest posts under the Minister of Defense correspond roughly to the respective group's population share: 56 percent of them are Shi'a Arab, 26 percent of them are Sunni Arab, and 7 percent are Kurd (9.75 percent are of unknown affiliation), yet there were, and remain, political attempts by the Prime Minister's office to increase pro-Shi'influence .[10]

Considering that almost all of these officials served in the pre-war military and were overwhelmingly Sunni Arab, this means that the small pre-war share of Shi'a officers now benefits from the need for more Shi'a visibility. Rapid promotion of middle rank Shi'a officers might thus explain the understaffing in this section of the Iraqi military. Furthermore, the rapid advance of the Shi'a creates resentment among some Sunni Arab officers and has essentially the same effect as a quota, namely calling meritocratic principles into question.

Both the Iraqi and the Lebanese cases highlight the desire for ethnically balanced armed forces in a post-conflict setting and the politically motivated attempts to achieve this goal that frequently forego moral concerns. The importance of a legitimate force accepted in all sectors of society is further stressed by the continuity of staff in both cases. Thus, policymakers involved in rebuilding armed forces in a multiethnic setting should aim for a fair balance of all ethnic groups within the military and pay close attention to nondiscrimination for all groups. The key issue here is, however, the institutionalization of ethnicity as a category within the armed forces.

The military needs hierarchy, meritocracy, and cohesion to function. Turning ethnic affiliation into a factor in the armed forces might backfire by infringing on the institution's proper functioning. Like no other organization, the armed forces rely on a set of certain structures and procedures that are unique and vital to its task. Rebalancing a military force according to ethnic affiliation might create intracorps jealousy, distorted chains of commands following the ethnic rather than the official order, fragile cohesion, and possibly disobedience.

A New Model Army? Recruiting the Right Soldiers.

While one rarely gets the chance to rebuild an armed force from zero, there is room for maneuvering on one important level, the recruitment of new personnel, be it in the officer corps or the rank and file. This level offers the opportunity to select staff according to a certain political outlook without meddling with existing structures and to choose politically untainted personnel. This level also offers the chance to create an ethnic balance early on.

Although Lebanon had toyed with the idea of an ethnic quota since the issue of Christian overrepresentation was raised in the 1960s, and had introduced such a quota in the early years of the civil war in 1978, the country only applied the quota rigorously after the civil war ended in 1990. Since then, officer cadets have been selected on a 50:50 quota basis. It is safe to assume that the higher ranks, which used to be disproportionally Christian, were equally balanced in the aftermath of the war. The problem with this quota is that it has introduced religion as a factor into an organization seeking cohesion and meritocratic principles and it is now very difficult to abolish. While the quota originally aimed at keeping Christians in check, it is now an advantage for them because young Christians apply in very low numbers to the officer corps. Nevertheless, it helped the Lebanese Army to overcome an image of partiality and bias and to present itself as a truly all-Lebanese institution. However, this also meant tapping into a pool of people who had potentially served in one of the militias; on average, 6.6 percent of draftees had done so. This was especially true in the early years after the conflict. [11]

Iraq has similar concerns, but has not yet decided on the creation of an ethnic quota in numerical terms. Article 9 of its constitution states that "the Iraqi armed forces will be composed of the components of the Iraqi people with due consideration given to their balance and representation without discrimination or exclusion."[12] Cadets are currently selected in an "ethnically fair" manner by a multiethnic board, as defined in the

General Secretariat Instruction 07/30797, dated September 4, 2008. Yet the instruction leaves room for interpretation—does it mean a fair balance of 33 percent for each group, or a percentage based on each group's strength? In practice, this means a repartition of approximately 60 percent Shi'a Arabs, 20 percent Sunni Arabs, and 18 percent Kurds, based on assumed ethnic shares in Iraq's population.

The debate about the ethnic make-up of the future Iraqi armed forces is ongoing, with some proposals offering a quota based on Iraq's 18 provinces.[13] This kind of quota would remove religious and ethnic considerations from the military as a state institution and avoid the institutionalization of religious affiliation as a recruitment criterion in the armed forces. Regionalizing the access to the officer corps thus seems a good way out of the ethnic trap while still calming fears of domination by any particular group.

The cases of both Lebanon and Iraq highlight the importance of ethnic balancing in the armed forces in a particularly challenging post-conflict situation. While it might not be desirable in military terms to introduce ethnicity, or a quota, into the armed forces' function, a way has to be found to alleviate fears of domination by one group. Thus, the very existence of a quota, especially an ethnic or religious one, reflects mutual fears in a very visible fashion.

While a quota can have the capacity to calm these fears, it should not be forgotten that there are limits to what such a system can do. Quotas usually can be circumvented and they fail to mobilize groups that are not interested in joining the armed forces. They only work in cases where there is a sufficient interest to join the military and this does not apply to the Sunni Arabs in either of the two cases.

Furthermore, there are several different applicable quotas. A religious or ethnic quota, for instance, can attempt to replicate the exact composition of society, or it can create an artificial balance that allocates equivalent shares to all groups present — as in the case of the Lebanese officer corps, which creates an artificial parity between Muslims and Christians that is nonexistent in reality.

The former is frequently difficult to implement not only because population numbers fluctuate (especially in a post-conflict scenario where there are displaced people, refugees, and returnees), but exact numbers are simply often not available — the last census in Lebanon took place in 1932, whereas the last census in Iraq of 1997 did not include questions related to ethnicity and religious affiliation (and did not cover the Kurdish regions).[14] Censuses are politically sensitive in multiethnic post-conflict countries, where numbers determine share in revenues, political seats, and possibly quotas. It is for this reason that no census is foreseeable in Lebanon despite significant debate, and that the upcoming one in Iraq will only ask for general religious affiliation (such as Muslim or Christian), but not for the specific sect.[15] Iraqi identification cards do not display the specific sect of the individual and no longer indicate the tribe, because this would give a certain indication of affiliation.

Allocating shares equally by group, in turn, imposes a certain vision of society that equates parity with equality — all groups, independently of their size, have the same rights in the state.[16] Quotas thus do not change social givens, but conceal them in public institutions so all groups can feel comfortable and equal. Interestingly, this kind of quota is generally only applied to the officer corps, whereas the rank and file remains open to interested parties. While the officer corps thus reflects an ideal image of society, the rank and file replicates the real interest in the armed forces, and the state for that matter, as an employer. Either way, a religious or ethnic quota inevitably opens up a vicious circle that constantly reaffirms a concept that essentially contradicts the idea of an overarching national identity, which is why calls for its abolishment are frequent in Lebanon, mostly voiced by Muslim groups who are generally more interested in joining the officer corps than Christians.

The main problem with ethnic and religious quotas in these cases is that they undermine the principle of merit. This is especially detrimental in the military. Strong hierarchies need strong meritocratic principles in order to be accepted. Quotas could jeopardize the respect of hierarchies, which is an important feature of military organizations.

Ethnic or religious quotas are a quick solution to a problem that needs further thinking. Regional quotas seem preferable to quotas based on a certain affiliation because they not only dilute the impact of ethnicity and religion on the armed forces, but also draw attention back to one common denominator all inhabitants of that particular country share: the homeland. One example that reconciles the desire for balance with a desire for meritocratic principles is a U.S. military recruitment scheme: by creating regional recruitment stations that have to fulfill certain recruitment quotas based on the propensity to enlist, a de facto regional quota is created, which in turn ensures recruitment of the best soldiers for the armed forces.

This idea seems quite popular in Iraq at the moment and might receive parliamentary approval in the near future.[17] The introduction of a regional rather than an ethnic or religious quota would also strengthen Iraqi nationalist forces in and out of the military. In spite of its diversity and supposedly artificial creation in the 1920s, Iraq has always seen a rather strong Iraqi nationalism strongly rooted in the pre-World War I decade and particularly virulent in the armed forces.[18]

The very name "Iraq" figured in Ottoman documents in the decade preceding the official emergence of the state, while people living on the banks of the Euphrates and Tigris had an understanding of a construct called Iraq that encompassed the provinces of Baghdad, Basra, and Mosul (which were not, as is frequently claimed, homogenous in either ethnic or religious terms). Thus, Iraqi nationalism exists and is based on a strong sense of territorial identity on the part of Iraq's inhabitants.[19]

States with a strong territorial identity, such as the United States, Iraq, Lebanon, or Germany tend to be diverse in religious or ethnic terms. These states might be better off with a regional quota since such a quota reaffirms the territorial dimension that is not only crucial to the state as such, but also to the identity that holds it all together, rather than being divisive. Furthermore, regional quotas tend to work better with federalist structures rather than centralist ones.

A New Beginning? Inclusion and Exclusion of Politically Compromised Personnel.

Post-conflict states face a particular challenge in the reconstruction process that requires delicate handling: the treatment of society's members that have compromised themselves, such as former regime members and militias. The most prominent example of this is the de-Nazification process in post-1945 Germany.

While the goal of a purged society and government free from politically compromised personnel might be a noble one, it is sometimes difficult to implement. Elites, whether politically tainted or not, usually carry the know-how, the intellectual capacity, and the institutional memory necessary to rebuild a state and its institutions. Excluding them from the rebuilding process can not only slow down the process, but also create a pool of frustrated personnel opposing the new state.

The same is true for the disbandment of former militias: while politically desirable because they infringe on the state's monopoly of violence and usually have committed illegal acts of bloodshed, the existence of large numbers of unemployed young people trained in weapons is not a risk easily taken. Rebuilding states thus have to choose between moral and practical considerations. Both Iraq and Lebanon offer useful insights in the way they handled these aspects.

During its 15-year civil war, Lebanon had seen a large number of militias and a substantial portion of the population served in them. Lebanon therefore passed a law in March 1991 granting amnesty for all political crimes committed prior to its enactment. In practice, this meant that virtually none of the militia leaders (except for *Forces Libanaises* [Lebanese Forces] leader Samir Geagea) were judged and tried for the acts committed during the civil war.

As for the militias, all except for one (Hezbollah) were disbanded, and 4,000 former militia members were integrated into the Lebanese Army; several former militia leaders joined parliament as political leaders. Lebanon has thus embarked on a "don't ask, don't tell" policy that annuls the past in order to move into a brighter future, and a purge of Lebanese society has not taken place.

However, this social amnesia is not complete, a fact that is especially visible in the armed forces. When the Lebanese Army integrated 4,000 ex-militia members, it proceeded in a decidedly biased manner, not only picking the lowest and least politicized ranks, but also excluding in its near-entirety the biggest Christian militia of the Lebanese Forces, which had applied for integration of 8,600 rank- and-file and 100 officers.[20] The large majority of the integrated group was from the Druze party militia and the Shi'a militia, Amal.

The reason for this bias was a political one: not only had the Lebanese Forces styled themselves as a rivaling Christian Maronite military, but they had also violently clashed with the Lebanese Army during the last years of the war. When the Lebanese Army thus decided to not only reject almost the entire list of Lebanese Forces candidates but also mistreated the 100 men that they nominally accepted (and who subsequently left the armed forces[21]), they made a choice that stood in stark contrast with the official policy of amnesty and amnesia. As an institution of the state, the Lebanese Army could not forgive the one militia that had lobbied for the cantonalization of Lebanon and had openly questioned the authority of the military, but it could accept personnel from militias that were not in competition with the Lebanese Army.

So far, the Lebanese case is one of official reconciliation and unofficial discrimination of those who had compromised themselves during the war. The case in Iraq is quite different, where there was, and is, an official purge policy, but one that has not been implemented to the degree that some would want it to be. De facto, this means that there is a solid continuity between the pre- and post-2003 Iraqi army.

While initial debaathification foresaw the removal of several thousand soldiers from the security forces and other governmental posts, this policy changed in April 2004 with the return of some senior ex-Baathists who were allowed to help strengthen the re-emergent officer corps.[22] This policy has been pursued by successive Iraqi governments, eventually leading to a rather large return of former Iraqi army members. An estimated 70 percent of the current officer corps (approximately 19,000) served in the pre-2003 armed forces, and probably every general had done so as well.[23] The same is true, though to a lesser extent, for the enlisted personnel, who are allowed back if their absence did not exceed 5 years. Considering that their retirement age is lower and their dismissal less precarious, one can assume that the number of returnees in the rank-and-file is lower.

The Law on Military Service and Pension mirrors the continuity of pre- and post-2003 armed forces well: not only does it stipulate that pensions be calculated based on the entire period served in the Iraqi military (pre- and post-2003), it also excludes returning officers from age limits.[24] There is thus a legal basis for the return of a significant number of former military. While this is beneficial from a seniority and expertise perspective, it also impedes Iraqi armed forces training and renewal efforts. Furthermore, debaathification appears to have been pursued less vigorously against Shi'a Baathists than against Sunnis, fuelling antagonism between these ethnic groups.[25]

When it comes to the militias, the landscape is much more diversified in Iraq than in Lebanon. A variety of organizations, differing in history, outlook, and relationship with the state, continued to infringe the state's monopoly of violence before and after 2003.

Some, such as the Kurdish Peshmerga or the Shi'a Badr Organization, existed well before 2003 and opposed the Baathi regime. Others, such as the Mahdi army, were created after the end of Saddam Hussein's regime and opposed the U.S. presence in Iraq, while the Sunni Sons of Iraq joined to fight Al-Qaida in Iraq.

There is thus no uniform treatment when it comes to Iraqi militias. Some, such as the Kurdish Peshmerga, are considered a lawful military force, and service in them will be recognized by the Iraqi military.[26] Some, such as the Wolf Brigade or the Special Police Commandos, form a part of Iraq's security structure. Some, such as the Mahdi army, are keen to remain separate from the state's institutions. However, others, such as the Sons of Iraq, seek integration into the armed forces even though some of their members used to be part of the insurgency. Their integration into the security forces was rather limited—only 25,000 of 90,000 Sons of Iraq fighters having been offered jobs in the security structures, which allegedly motivated some to rejoin the insurgency. On the other hand, Kurdish units based on Peshmerga structures were successfully integrated into the new military force, mostly clustered in the 2nd Division, which, along with another mostly Kurdish division, is the only one being rotated throughout the country.[27] The professional outlook of the Peshmerga, who consider themselves a professional military force, has probably helped their integration into the Iraqi armed forces in spite of historical clashes between the two forces. This double standard on the part of the government might backfire one day.[28]

There are several conclusions that can be drawn from this analysis. First of all, moral concerns are usually outweighed by practical concerns of social peace and reconstruction efforts. Exclusion of experienced yet politically undesirable personnel not only decapitates the military leadership, it also creates a potentially dangerous group of discontented people. In order to uphold a rhetoric of change, the reintegration of these personnel should ideally be accompanied by cosmetic measures, such as personnel turnover in the most visible ranks, so as to gain public approval. A rhetoric of reconciliation seems more effective than one of punishment and purge, while the trial of top personnel might be sufficient to allay moral concerns.

As for the integration of militias, this approach seems to have limits from an institutional perspective: large intakes of soldiers that have fought against the armed forces is usually resisted by the organization itself, introducing an element of politicization and lack of professionalism. Flawed integration programs in both Lebanon and Iraq chose to select only a few low-ranking soldiers, running the risk of leaving a pool of unemployed people willing to use violence. Inclusion or exclusion of politically undesirable personnel is always a delicate choice to make, but the decision ultimately depends on the target society and its capacity for reconciliation.

The Cradle of the New State? Public Image of the New Military.

Conflict affects the armed forces in more than one way. Among other things, it strains the military's image in the eyes of the larger society. Accused of violence against civilians, of collaboration with the enemy, or of passivity, the military frequently needs to redefine its relationship with society. Because the new state and its institutions need public approval and trust, especially in the security sector, this matters greatly to post-conflict reconstruction.

18

In the case of the Lebanese Army, this relationship is marked first by the army's striving to be a national symbol, and second by its rather unsuccessful record during the civil war years. Still, the army has managed to present itself as a widely-accepted symbol of interethnic cooperation and a peaceful Lebanon. This assessment might be surprising, since the military had to stay passive during the war and had not participated in any of the wars against Israel after the battle of Malikiyya in 1948. Thus, one can assume that the positive image[29] that the army enjoys across Lebanese society is not linked to its military achievements. An analysis of the Lebanese media, however, shows clearly that the Lebanese Army continued to receive positive news coverage throughout the war, even in 1984, its year of disintegration. Elements that marked its portrayal that year included adjectives such as legitimate, unitary, heroic, and trustworthy.[30] This image remained intact until today throughout society and the media, with the armed forces being perceived as the vanguard of unity and the embodiment of national identity.[31]

This becomes apparent in the results of a survey: 41.7 percent of Lebanese agree with the statement, "Lebanese trust the state and its institutions," while almost twice as many, 75.3 percent, agree with the statement, "Lebanese trust their army."[32] More importantly, this positive image is constant throughout all sectors of Lebanese society, ranging from 65.4 percent among Maronites (who trust their state by 15.5 percent only) to 80.6 percent among Shi'a Muslims (who trust the state by 43.7 percent). In spite of technical shortcomings, the Lebanese Army thus not only enjoys a rather positive image, it has also turned into a symbol for post-conflict reconciliation and transethnic cooperation.[33]

While the Iraqi Army used to be a similar symbol for Iraqi nationalism and its officers constituted part of the country's elite, this image has crumbled since the first Gulf War. Considered successful against Iran, and arguably the most politicized armed force in the Middle East (the first ones to intervene in politics in 1936), members of the armed forces constituted a part of the country's elite—in the 1970s, young women would state that they would "marry an army officer or not marry at all."[34] Although the Baath party and Saddam Hussein managed to establish a tight grip over the armed forces, those forces were not Hussein's favored tool of suppression within and outside Iraq. Rather, he created a complex system of different organizations, such as the Fedayin Saddam and the Republican Guard, to bolster his power. The military's reputation started to wane with the defeat in 1991 and the effect the international sanctions had on its staff. Rather than standing for Iraqi nationalism and a transethnic outlook, the Iraqi military lost its good standing as its image became intermingled with that of a brutal regime that suppressed dissidents and antagonists.

With the disbandment and reconstruction of the Iraqi armed forces in 2003, an opportunity arose for the institution to reinvent its relationship with society. However, this relationship remains blurred and at times contradictory, as much as the military's identity does.

As in the Lebanese case, the Iraqi Army is not perceived as an effective provider of security—only 46 percent of Iraqis consider it to be effective in the maintenance of security. However, 70 percent of Iraqis declare that they feel secure when they see the Iraqi Army in their neighborhood. There is thus a trust in the Iraqi Army that remains difficult to explain — although rated mediocre when it comes to security, they rate especially high when compared to other groups, such as militias, tribes, and U.S. forces, when Iraqis state that they have the highest confidence (85 percent) in the Iraqi Army.[35] Several explanations are possible for this gap between actual security provision and the positive image.

The Iraqi Army, just as the Lebanese Army, embodies the legitimacy of the state, as opposed to the militias who embody the break-down of state authority. Furthermore, it represents the ideal unitary outlook of Iraq as a multiethnic country. These elements, rather than its actual work as a security provider, are what make up the image of an armed force in a post-conflict situation, especially in a multiethnic society. It is for this reason that application rates for the Iraqi Army, especially the officer corps, remain high throughout all ethnic groups, and it is for precisely this reason that the insurgents target groups waiting in front of recruiting stations or use Iraqi Army uniforms when perpetrating their acts: discrediting the Iraqi military enhances militia rule.

For an outside force, this not only means that it is important to strengthen the national outlook of the armed forces, it also means that the stronger the image of the military in society, the stronger the ability of the military to actually disarm and dismantle militias. What enabled the Lebanese Army to impose itself as the national institution was its public image as the only legal force in the country, as opposed to the sectarian militias. It is important to note, however, that there is a difference between the image and actuality. While the Lebanese Army has a good reputation, it is nevertheless powerless when opposing the Israeli

Army, has coexisted for a long time with the Syrian Army, and still coexists with Hezbollah. As we have seen, the same is true for the Iraqi Army. By implication, this means that when rebuilding an armed force, immaterial elements, such as its image and discourse, are as important as material ones. While sectarianism might be manipulated in both the Iraqi and the Lebanese military, their image as a transethnic, legal force is an important precondition for other crucial steps related to the post-conflict reconstruction process. The image of an impartial, balanced, and legal armed force will not only help recruit the right personnel from all sectors of society, but will also create an ambiance of security that will help build up infrastructure and encourage investment. Security, like prosperity, is more about perception than reality.

Thus, the Lebanese Army embarked on a public relations campaign, including spots on TV and billboards, presenting itself as the only truly national institution guaranteeing Lebanon's existence as a nation and country. The gap between effectiveness and image, in both cases, is so intriguing that one has to wonder if it is the social recognition that eventually gives the armed forces the power to assume full control of the security sector rather than the other way around. While military effectiveness can be measured in several ways, its rooting in society cannot be underestimated, with the legitimacy of the armed forces being key in a post-conflict setting.

Training, Training, Training:
How to Professionalize the New Force.

Military professionalism is crucial to the functioning of the armed forces. It determines the commitment, skill, and discipline of the individual soldiers and is an antidote to many problems that plague post-conflict countries, such as military intervention in politics, mutiny, and disintegration. But while military professionalism is desperately needed in a post-conflict situation, it has usually been adversely affected by the conflict years, especially when there was widespread sectarianism that tested loyalties and cohesion. Not only has the organization often suffered from fractured chains of command, understaffing in critical posts, lowering of educational standards, equipment shortfalls, personnel issues, and damaged infrastructure, its monopoly on violence has usually been challenged by one or several militias. How much its professionalism has been affected also depends on such pre-conflict factors as professional satisfaction, length of service, *esprit de corps*, social recognition, leadership, and sense of duty.

The professionalism of both the Iraqi and Lebanese militaries were tested, and both organizations attempted to reestablish professionalism in several ways. Professionalism in the armed forces is generally characterized by four elements: dedication to service, expertise, responsibility, and corporate culture. The military's client is the nation; the profession is a whole way of life that encompasses all areas. It is thus more than "just a job," more than an occupation.[36] The problem with professionalism is that it can only partly be influenced by outsiders. Some of its most important elements, such as dedication and responsibility, are ultimately rooted in the military's relationship with society — depending on that relationship, professionalism will be easier or less easy to rebuild.

The Lebanese Army had a solid basis to build on once the civil war came to an end. While it had suffered from infrastructural damage and loss of weapons to the militias (through theft and illegal selling), it maintained a comparatively strong professionalism throughout the early war years largely based on its noninvolvement in the conflict itself. While this professionalism was eroded first by passive on-looking (a whole Shi'a brigade left the army in 1984, 7 years after the war had started) and personalization under the commander in chief, Major General Michel Awn, there was nevertheless a rather strong professional background that could be, and was, revived once the conflict ended.

A force priding itself on a long-standing tradition of military professionalism concentrated in the ideology of *Shehabism* (named after its first commander in chief, Fuad Shehab) advocating the military's aloofness from sectarianism and politics, it had a narrative on hand to revive the discourse of the Lebanese Army as a professional force focusing on duty and task.[37] Intensifying training and educational courses, the Lebanese Army managed to reinstitutionalize professionalism in two senses: in its official discourse and self-perception. The military took on the function of acting as a symbol of national unity, stressing its multiethnic composition as the prime connection to its client, the Lebanese nation. Secondly, it improved cohesion not only through the reshuffling of the brigades, but mostly by buttressing this measure with intense training classes to make the troops understand its purpose and importance.

Although ill-equipped and underfunded, the Lebanese Army nevertheless proved its professionalism and cohesion in a large-scale purge of Islamist fighters hidden in Palestinian refugee camps in 2007, and is considered to be a professional, cohesive force by

Lebanese and foreigners alike. Lebanese Army professionalism can thus be seen as rather strong.

The Iraqi Army likewise emerged from the decades of dictatorship with its professionalism seriously eroded. Despite its traditionally strong national and professional outlook— Iraqi Army unit cohesion was rather good throughout 60 years of conflict[38]—the regime's interference with the organization's functioning tainted its professionalism fundamentally. Overall political meddling and large-scale Baathification of the officer corps undermined morale; challenged traditional lines of authority; circumvented hierarchy and promotional systems; and introduced cronyism, sectarianism, and tribal elements into an institution that prided itself on Iraqi and Arab nationalism.[39] Saddam Hussein elevated himself to the rank of general and then field marshal without his ever having served a day in the armed forces, changed the army's traditions, and created an overall sentiment of animosity within the officer corps. Most importantly, he undermined professional basics of the armed forces over 3 decades while institutionalizing iron discipline that crumbled once he fell from power.

It is thus not surprising that the new Iraqi Army emerged challenged on the professional front. Leadership, cohesion, sense of duty to nation and institution were, and still are, missing to some extent as a result of decades of dictatorship. Leadership qualities, for instance, were dangerous in a system where they could be perceived as a threat to the regime—assertive personnel, especially in the officer middle ranks, are thus missing.[40] Cohesion in multiethnic units remains fragile, due in part to a large and rapid intake of new troops that had been out of the force for several years, missing leadership, and political interference with units that remain posted in one area. Moving battalions across divisions could enhance a national feeling, remove political patronage, and strengthen cohesion. [41] Desertion rates reach 40 percent in areas that are difficult and possibly deadly, indicating a low sense of duty, which might not be surprising given very short basic training of 3 to 5 weeks. This lack of training cannot be made up by the mere fact that most soldiers served in the old Iraqi Army as well, since experience as such is only one element of professionalism.[42]

Although the Iraqi Army has been supported on several levels both by NATO's Training Mission and the U.S. Training and Assistance Mission, one crucial element is missing that neither international funds nor expertise can provide—the glue that holds it all together, the national ideology that used to constitute the Iraqi Army's backbone, has been severely affected by the sectarian events of 2004-06. An armed force that has no identity will have difficulty providing its staff with a sense of duty to nation and country, creating cohesion and commitment. While skill and discipline might be trainable, the nontangible elements of military professionalism have to come from within society and the institution in order to be sufficiently powerful.

Because Iraqi army officers played an important part in the emergence and development of Iraqi nationalism at the beginning of the 20th century, there is an historical basis to return to. Idealizing the unity of nation and military, and the role of the latter in the formation of the former, the Iraqi military had, and possibly still has, potential for nation-building as it did in the heyday of Sati al-Husri and the German military thinkers.[43] Thus, there is reason to believe that (a) the Iraqi army can resume this role, and (b) there is institutional memory in the military itself that can be revived for this purpose.

Professionalization of a military force relies on several elements that need time, funds, and an intrinsic inner logic in order to be effective. These are a sense of purpose, a sense of duty, and a sense of belonging to a nation. These require education, but must come primarily from within the military institution itself. It is for this reason that the military is frequently associated with nationalism, a force that is difficult to create from the outside. An armed force that has no devotion or sense of duty to its nation will find it very difficult to stand together in times of war and conflict regardless of the amount of training.

Conclusion.

Rebuilding armed forces is a task that needs funds, expertise, and determination. Mostly, it needs an understanding of the target society that will ultimately be not only the new military's client, but also its provider in terms of staff and funds. Embedded in society, and thus in the (post-) conflict, the reconstructed armed force faces societal challenges that must be taken into account when assisting and advising it.

Of particular importance is the ethnic or religious composition of the military. Wherever society's stratification has changed because of the conflict — or needs to change if peace is to be sustainable — the armed forces need to reflect this. Yet this is difficult to implement if the military relies on personnel from pre-conflict times who usually mirror the social stratification as it was before the war. Several choices need to be made that usually are difficult because they will jeopardize either the organization as such (by relying on inexperienced personnel, ostracizing former elites, or interfering with its procedures) or the peace (by keeping an armed force that resembles the "old days" and that, in turn, might not be trusted by the new government). The choice is delicate because both options contain an element of instability that the fragile post-conflict scenario does not need. More importantly, interfering with an existing body of troops is much more difficult than raising a new armed force from scratch. One option is to either dismiss members of the over-represented group or to hire soldiers from the under-represented group and fast-track them into higher positions. This approach, however, risks (a) creating a pool of weapon-trained personnel angry at the new regime (as happened in Iraq, where dismissed officers joined the insurgency), or (b) causing intra-corps jealousy against the newcomers and resentment against policymakers. Thus, neither option can be recommended.

More effective are cosmetic changes that satisfy both the public need for equality and the military's desire for noninterference in their affairs, such as creating an ethnic balance only at the most visible level of the military hierarchy, while keeping subordinate echelons untouched from ethnic considerations (such as in Iraq, where a largely Sunni officer corps is headed by a carefully balanced upper echelon).

Interference with the armed forces' ethnic or religious make-up is much easier during recruitment and will be less resented by the military if meritocratic principles are combined with a quota, for instance based on regional origin, ethnicity, or religious affiliation. The latter two risk introducing into the institution ethnic and religious criteria that are traditionally at odds with its nonsectarian outlook and have a tendency to perpetuate themselves. If meritocratic and transparent principles are applied, however, accusations of patronage and corruption can be prevented to some extent.

The actual make-up of the military can be further influenced by the exclusion of politically compromised personnel or the inclusion of militias that usually emerge during internal conflicts. Purging soldiers that have occupied key positions before or during the conflict, but are associated with the old regime and thus are politically undesirable, is a delicate matter. Because of their expertise, network of contact, and their dangerous potential level of frustration, the military frequently has to overlook moral considerations and focus on practical aspects. Decapitating the armed forces' senior ranks means leaving an institution void of experienced leadership, which will have an immediate impact on operational capability. Likewise, the inclusion of former militias into the armed forces will introduce an element of politicization and lack of professionalism that is usually resented by the institution itself. Flawed integration programs in both Lebanon and Iraq chose to select only a few low-ranking personnel, leaving a pool of unemployed troops willing to use violence. Again, the choice remains a dilemma, with potential dangers looming on both sides.

A less controversial area for decisionmakers concerns the image of the armed forces in post-conflict society, itself in dire need of symbols of peaceful coexistence and nationalism. The military is not only well-suited for this symbolic post, it is frequently also the only institution left that can embody peaceful cooperation. The Lebanese Army is a good example of a post-conflict force that has gained esteem throughout society for its symbolic value rather than for its actual military achievements. It is difficult to measure this impact on society, but there is an important stabilizing element in public approval of an institution that symbolizes not only the state and its monopoly of violence, but also interethnic peace and cooperation. More importantly, public benevolence will decidedly increase the military's room for maneuver.

Lastly, the military's professionalism is directly linked to its image in society. The more professional and aloof from society's problems the armed forces are, the more likely they are not only to operate properly, but also to be esteemed by the population. Training and education as such will not suffice to achieve that, but a nationalistic ideology emphasizing the important mission and devotion of the military to society is vital for it. This, however, is difficult to achieve by an outside advisory force. Rather, it has to come from within the institution, driven by an intrinsic desire to serve country and people. Without this spiritual element, the armed forces will have difficulty achieving cohesion and leadership.

In a post-conflict situation, policymakers frequently have to make harsh decisions when it comes to the new military force. In order to balance the pros and cons appropriately, an intimate knowledge of the target society and its military institution is crucial if years of investment both in budgetary and personnel terms are to be well-placed.

A mere focus on technical aspects will not suffice to overcome the issues a post-conflict force faces. Such elements as ethnicity, nationalism, or professionalism are crucial, yet also more difficult to address. However, both the cases of Iraq and of Lebanon give us insights into how a military force might tackle these challenges and reemerge as the legitimate and trusted armed force of the country.

ENDNOTES

1. Ahmed Hashim, "Saddam Husayn and Civil-Military Relations in Iraq: The Quest for Legitimacy and Power," *Middle East Journal*, Vol. 57, No. 1, Winter 2003, p. 38.

2. Ahmed al-Zaini, *Al-bina al-maanawi lil-quwat al-musallaha al-iraqya* (*The Building of Cohesion in the Iraqi Armed Forces*), Baghdad, Iraq: Afaq Arabya Publishing House, 2000.

3. Iskandar Ghanem, *Revue Al-Hawadess* (*Periodical Incidents*), May 7, 1976, No. 1017, p. 14.

4. Andre Rondé, "L'Armée libanaise et la restauration de l'Etat de droit" (The Lebanese Army and the Reconstruction of a State of Rights"), *Revue Droit et Defense*, No. 2, 1998, p. 30.

5. Michael Bauer, *Training the Iraqi Air Force: Lessons from a U.S. C-130 Advisory Mission*, Policy Focus #73, Washington, DC: The Washington Institute for Near East Policy, August 2007, p. 11.

6. International Institute for Strategic Studies, *The Military Balance 2010*, London, UK: Routledge, 2010, p. 235.

7. Sharon Otterman, *Iraq: Debaathification*, New York: Council on Foreign Relations, April 7, 2005, available from *www.cfr. org/publication/7853/iraq.html?id=7853 #p3*; Tim Pearce, "Iraq Pushes on With Reinstating Saddam-era troops," *Reuters.com*, February 26, 2010, available from *www.reuters.com/article/idUS-TRE61P45F20100226*.

8. "Sunni role in military in Iraq falls short of goal," *The Washington Times*, January 24, 2005, available from *www.washington-times.com/news/2005/jan/24/20050124-121258-7555r/?page=1*.

9. Interview conducted by the author with NATO Training Mission Iraq Personnel, Baghdad, July 27, 2010; *The Military Balance 2008*, p. 228; Barak A. Salmoni, "Iraq's Unready Security Forces: an Interim Assessment," *Middle East Review of International Affairs*, Vol. 8, No. 3, September 2004, p. 23.

10. Kenneth Katzman, *Iraq: Post-Saddam Governance and Security*, Washington, DC: Congressional Research Service, 2008, p. 32.

11. *"Au Liban, les anciens miliciens se reconvertissent dans l'armée,"* ("In Lebanon, former militias convert into the army"), *La Libération,* April 14, 1995.

12. Republic of Iraq, National Security Advisory Council of Ministers, "Iraqi Constitution," *Iraqi National Security Strategy 2007-2010,* Annex I, p. 4.

13. Interview conducted by the author with Iraqi military personnel, Baghdad, June 10, 2010.

14. United Nations, "Press briefing on Iraq Demographics," August 8, 2003, available from *www.un.org/News/briefings/docs/2003/iraqdemobrf.doc.htm.*

15. Jim Loney, "Iraq to hold first full census since '87 in October," *Reuters.com*, January 16, 2010, available from *www.reuters.com/article/idUSTRE60F0ZL20100116.*

16. Florence Gaub, *Military Integration after Civil Wars*, New York: Routledge, 2010, pp. 122-125.

17. Interview conducted by the author with Iraqi military personnel, Baghdad, June 10, 2010.

18. Ofra Bengio, *Saddam's Word*, Cambdrige, UK: Oxford University Press, 2002, pp. 91-93.

19. Reidar Visser, "Centralism and Unitary State Logic in Iraq: from Midhat Pasha to Jawad al-Maliki: A Continous Trend?" April 22, 2006, available from *www.historiae.org/maliki.asp.*

20. Elizabath Picard, *The Demobilization of the Lebanese Militias*, Oxford, UK: Centre for Lebanese Studies, 1999, pp. 6-8.

21. Interview conducted by the author with former *Forces Libanaises* Fighter, Beirut, Lebanon, April 21, 2004.

22. Otterman, p. 3.

23. Interview conducted by the author with NATO Training Mission Iraq Personnel, Baghdad, Iraq, June 7, 2010.

24. *Military Service and Pension Law*, Articles 4, 5, 10, and 34, Baghdad, Iraq: Republic of Iraq, 2009.

25. *The Next Iraqi War?* Middle East Report No. 52, Brussels, Belgium: International Crisis Group, p. 10.

26. *Military Service and Pension Law*, Article 39.

27. *The Military Balance 2010*, p. 228.

28. Thomas S. Mowle, "Iraq's Militia Problem," *Survival*, Vol. 48, No. 3, October 2006, p. 48.

29. *L'Orient le Jour*, "Honneur à l'armée! Honneur de l'armée" ("Honour to the Army! Honour of the Army!"), May 27, 2000; *L'Orient le Jour*, "Armée — Un corps uni, après avoir été un puzzle. De 1976 à 1998, les étapes d'une renaissance" ("The Army — a united body after having been a puzzle. From 1976 to 1998, the steps of a rebirth"), November 24, 1998.

30. Najah Abdallah, "L'image de l'armée libanaise à travers de la presse quotidienne au Liban en 1984" ("The image of the Lebanese Army via the daily press in Lebanon in 1984"), Ph.D. diss., University Michel de Montaigne, Bordeaux III, 1992, pp. 188-191, 207, 252, 284.

31. Hamid Iskandar, "L'évolution de l'image der l'armée libanaise 1990-2000" ("The evolution of the Lebanese Army's image 1990-2000"), Ph.D. diss., University Paris II Panthéon-Assas, 2002, pp. 338-367; "In a Political Move, Lebanon offers an Army that All of its Sects Can Accept: Its Own," *The New York Times*, August 14, 2006.

32. Fabiola Azar and Etienne Mullet, "Muslims and Christians in Lebanon: Common Views on Political Issues," *Journal of Peace Research*, No. 11, 2002, p. 741.

33. Florence Gaub, "Multiethnic armies in the aftermath of civil war: Lessons learned from Lebanon," *Defence Studies*, Vol. 7, No. 1, March 2007, pp. 5-20.

34. Interview conducted by the author with Iraqi historian, Baghdad, Iraq, July 22, 2010.

35. *Measuring Stability and Security in Iraq*, Report to Congress In accordance with the Department of Defense Supplemental Act 2008 Section 9204, Public Law 110-252, Washington, DC: Department of Defense, December 2009, pp. 34-35.

36. Reserve Officers Training Corps, Military Science and Leadership Program, Course 101, "Leadership and Personal Development," Section L07, available from *www.scribd.com/doc/6176648/MSL-101-L07-Officer-Ship-and-the-Army-Profession.*

37. Marwan Harb, "Le Chehabisme ou les limites d'une expérience de modernisation politique au Liban" ("Shehabisme or the limits of a political modernisation experience in Lebanon"), Master's Thesis, Université Saint Joseph, Beirut, Lebanon, November 2007.

38. Kenneth M. Pollack, *Arabs at War: Military Effectiveness, 1948-1991*, Lincoln, NE: University of Nebraska Press, 2002, p. 266.

39. Hashim, pp. 28-29; Andrew Parasiliti and Sinan Antoon, "Friends in Need, Foes to Heed: The Iraqi Military in Politics," *Middle East Policy*, Vol. 7, No. 4, October 2000, p. 134.

40. William Bache, "Transferring American Military Values to Iraq," *The Middle East Review of International Affairs*, Vol. 11, No. 3, September 2007, p. 2; Special Inspector General for Iraq Reconstruction (SIGIR), *Quarterly Report to the United States Congress*, Public Law 108-106, as amended, and Public Law 95-452, Washington, DC: U.S. Congress, January 31, 2010, p. 43.

41. Najim Abed Al-Jabouri, "Iraqi Security Forces After U.S. Troop Withdrawal: An Iraqi Perspective," *Strategic Forum*, No. 245, August 2009, p. 1; Tim Arango, "Iraq's Forces Prove Able, but Loyalty Is Uncertain," *The New York Times*, April 13, 2010, avail-

able from *www.nytimes.com/2010/04/14/world/middleeast/14security. html*; Aqeel Hussein and Colin Freeman, "Iraqi Army Forces Defect to Moqtada al-Sadr," *Telegraph*, March 30, 2008, available from *www.telegraph.co.uk/news/worldnews/1583329/Iraqi-army-forces-defect-to-Moqtada-al-Sadr.html*; Steven Lee Myers, "Concerns Mount on Preparedness of Iraq's Forces," *The New York Times*, May 8, 2009, available from *www.nytimes.com/2009/05/08/world/ middleeast/08security.html*.

42. Carl D. Grunow, "Advising Iraqis: Building the Iraqi Army," *Military Review*, July-August 2006, pp. 8-17.

43. Phebe Marr, "The Development of a Nationalist Ideology in Iraq, 1920-1941," *The Muslim World*, Vol. 75, Issue 2, 1985, pp. 85-101.

www.ingramcontent.com/pod-product-compliance
Lightning Source LLC
Chambersburg PA
CBHW060010300526
45794CB00003B/1158

* 9 7 8 1 4 7 8 1 1 3 3 9 3 *